OXFORD CHORAL SONGS

To Bobby

A Smuggler's Song

OCS 1222
Unison

RUDYARD KIPLING*

CHRISTOPHER LE FLEMING

If you wake at mid-night, and hear a hor-se's feet,
Run-ning round the wood-lump if you chance to find

* Reprinted by permission
A two-part version of this song is also published (T45).

Bran - dy for the Par - son, 'Bac - cy for the Clerk;

cresc. - - - - - -

La - ces for a la - dy; let - ters for a spy, ___

pp

And watch the wall, my darl - ing, while the Gen - tle - men go

1st time   2nd time

by!

(in time)

If you do as you've been told, 'like - ly there's a chance,

You'll be give a dain - ty doll, — all the way from France, With a

cap of Va - len - ci - ennes, and a vel - vet hood— A pre - sent from the Gen - tle - men, a -

-long o' be - ing good! Five and twen - ty po - nies,

Reproduced and printed by
Halstan & Co. Ltd., Amersham, Bucks., England

OXFORD UNIVERSITY PRESS

1.95

FLEMIN...

A Smuggler's Song

OCS 1222

ISBN 0-19-340755